FAMOUS
Native North Americans

Bobbie Kalman & Molly Aloian
Crabtree Publishing Company
www.crabtreebooks.com

FAMOUS
Native North Americans

Created by Bobbie Kalman

Dedicated by Molly Aloian
For my big sister Lisa—my favorite person to laugh with

Editor-in-Chief
Bobbie Kalman

Writing team
Bobbie Kalman
Molly Aloian

Substantive editor
Niki Walker

Editors
Amanda Bishop
Rebecca Sjonger
Kathryn Smithyman

Art director
Robert MacGregor

Design
Margaret Amy Reiach

Production coordinator
Heather Fitzpatrick

Photo research
Crystal Foxton
Laura Hysert

Digital prepress
Embassy Graphics

Printer
Worzalla Publishing

Consultant
Bruce E. Johansen, Frederick W. Kayser Professor, Communication and Native American Studies, University of Nebraska at Omaha

Photographs and reproductions
AP/Wide World Photos: page 29
Arthur K. Miller/Art Asylum: page 30
Private Collection/Bridgeman Art Library: pages 20, 21 (top)
Glenbow Archives: NA-2631-2, page 18
The Granger Collection, New York: front cover, pages 8, 10, 11, 12, 14, 16, 17 (top), 26, 31
The Greenwich Workshop, Inc. Shelton, CT: © Howard Terpning: *Chief Joseph Rides to Surrender* (detail), page 19; *The Ghost Dance* (detail), page 25
© Permission of Lewis Parker: pages 6, 7 (bottom)
National Archives of Canada, Ottawa: (Accession No. 1984-45-269), page 23
National Gallery of Canada, Ottawa, Transfer from the Canadian War Memorials, 1921: page 13 (top)
Artwork from PicturesNow.com: pages 9, 13 (bottom), 15, 21 (bottom)
R.C. Gorman's Navajo Gallery: *Night Stories*, page 28
Rob Dewall: Crazy Horse 1/34th Scale Model, page 17 (bottom)
Rochester Museum & Science Center, Rochester, New York: page 24
© Superstock: pages 1, 7 (top)
Vancouver Public Library, Special Collections: 9429 (detail), page 27
Other images by Circa: Art/Image Club Graphics

Illustrations
Barbara Bedell: pages 5, 29, 31
Katherine Kantor: border
Margaret Amy Reiach: page 27
Bonna Rouse: pages 6, 22

Crabtree Publishing Company
www.crabtreebooks.com   1-800-387-7650

PMB 16A
350 Fifth Avenue
Suite 3308
New York, NY
10118

612 Welland Avenue
St. Catharines
Ontario
Canada
L2M 5V6

73 Lime Walk
Headington
Oxford
OX3 7AD
United Kingdom

Cataloging-in-Publication Data
Kalman, Bobbie.
  Famous Native North Americans / Bobbie Kalman & Molly Aloian.
    p. cm. -- (Native nations of North America series)
Includes index.
Summary: Profiles Native Americans who made significant differences in the histories of their own nations, and in the history of the United States and Canada, as interpreters, guides, warriors, and peacemakers.
  ISBN 0-7787-0379-7 (RLB) -- ISBN 0-7787-0471-8 (pbk.)
  1. Indians of North America--Biography--Juvenile literature.
2. Indian women--North America--Biography--Juvenile literature. [1. Indians of North America--Biography. 2. Women--Biography.] I. Aloian, Molly. II. Title. III. Series.
  E89.K36 2004
  973.04'97'00922--dc22
                                          2003016193
                                          LC

Contents

Famous Native North Americans

Long before Europeans arrived in North America, hundreds of Native **nations**, or groups of Native people, lived on the lands that are now known as the United States and Canada. The people of these nations spoke different languages and had distinct cultures and traditions.

Resisting change

The Europeans brought great changes—and, often, hardships—to the lives of Native North Americans. Over time, several Native leaders became famous for resisting these changes. Some leaders became known for fearlessly defending their nations' **territories** or working to preserve their people's cultures, traditions, and languages. Others provided hope and guidance for their people in the changing world. These Native North Americans earned the respect and admiration of their people.

Past and present

The famous Native North Americans in this book are people from the past and present who are remembered today for various reasons. They were peace leaders, war leaders, spiritual leaders, intellectuals, **negotiators**, artists, and entertainers. No matter what their achievements were, they played important roles in the histories of their nations, as well as the histories of the United States and Canada.

*Some Native people are famous for helping European explorers and **settlers**, or people from other countries who claimed Native lands for themselves.*

Leading their people

The four Native leaders shown on this page are all famous for different achievements. Each man is from a different nation and territory.

(right) Gall was a chief of the Lakota (Sioux) nation. He became a war chief for the famous Lakota leader, Sitting Bull, during the 1870s. Turn to pages 16-17 to read more about Sitting Bull and his role in history.

(right) Chief Seath'tl was a wise leader of the Suquamish and Duamish nations. He often acted as their spokesman. He and his people lived in the area that is now Seattle, Washington. In the 1850s, Chief Seath'tl and his people surrendered their homelands to American settlers.

(above) Quanah Parker, a chief of the Comanche nation, is famous for protecting his nation's traditional territories in Texas. He and his warriors were eventually forced to surrender to the United States government in 1875.

(right) Washakie became a chief of the Shoshone nation during the 1840s. He was chief for over 60 years and is known for helping American settlers, traders, and trappers in the western United States.

Hiawatha and the Peacemaker

Hundreds of years before European settlers arrived, the Oneida, Cayuga, Onondaga, Seneca, and Mohawk nations lived in neighboring territories in the Great Lakes region of North America. The people of these five nations all spoke languages that belonged to the **Iroquoian** language group. According to their **oral tradition**, there was a time of great darkness when the five nations were in constant battle with one another. The violence saddened a man known today as the Peacemaker. He had a powerful vision of peace among these five nations and

was determined to make it a reality. The Peacemaker shared his vision with a Mohawk man named Hiawatha, who was a gifted and powerful speaker. Hiawatha offered to travel with the Peacemaker to the villages of the other nations to spread the message of unity. Together, the two men convinced the five nations that they could live together peacefully.

*Using a picture, Hiawatha showed how the positions of the territories of the five nations formed the shape of a **longhouse**. A longhouse was the traditional dwelling of the people of these nations. The five nations became known as the People of the Longhouse for these two reasons.*

Peace and prosperity

Hiawatha and the Peacemaker helped the people see that it was better to join together in friendship than to destroy one another. The nations agreed and buried all their weapons beneath a giant white pine tree, now known as the Tree of Peace. They called themselves Haudenosaunee and named their **alliance** the Haudenosaunee Confederacy. For hundreds of years, the Haudenosaunee have lived and worked together in peace. They continue to revere the person who brought them peace. Out of respect, his name is never spoken. He is always referred to as the Peacemaker. Today, the confederacy is known by several names, including the Iroquois Confederacy and the Iroquois League. It is also known as the Six Nations because the Tuscarora nation joined the alliance in the early 1700s.

Hiawatha is respected for bringing the Peacemaker's vision to life and acting as his spokesman.

A model for the Founding Fathers

The opinions and thoughts of all people were of equal importance in the Haudenosaunee Confederacy. The people were represented by chiefs who were chosen by the mothers of each nation's **clans**, or family groups. The chiefs stated the wishes of their people at **councils**. Today, the U.S. government is also made up of people who act as representatives. Many historians acknowledge that the Founding Fathers of the American government, including Benjamin Franklin, used the Haudenosaunee Confederacy as a model when drafting the United States **Constitution** in 1787.

The legend of Pocahontas

Pocahontas was born in present-day Virginia, sometime around 1595. She lived along Chesapeake Bay in a region now called the Tidewater. She belonged to a nation of **Algonkian** speakers known as Powhatans. Pocahontas's father, Chief Powhatan (Wahunsonacock), was the most powerful leader in the region.

The Europeans arrive

On April 26, 1607, more than one hundred British settlers sailed into Chesapeake Bay aboard three ships. The settlers established the first British **colony** in North America, which was an area ruled by Britain. They named the colony "Jamestown" after their king, James I. Captain John Smith was the leader of the colony. The colonists were not prepared for the harsh weather conditions in the new colony. During their first few months living in Jamestown, the settlers relied on the Powhatans and other nearby nations for food and other supplies. The Powhatans tried to live peacefully with the newcomers, but the colonists soon began taking over more land and demanding corn, beans, and other foods. When the Powhatans refused, the colonists stole food from them or forced them to trade for it. Relations between the Powhatans and the colonists soon became hostile.

The legend

In 1608, John Smith was captured by Pocahontas's uncle and taken to Chief Powhatan's village. According to legend, Powhatan warriors were about to kill Smith when Pocahontas saved him. Many historians doubt that Smith was ever in danger of dying. Instead, they believe that the Powhatans were performing a ritual to initiate Smith into their nation.

Taken hostage

Captain John Smith returned to England the following year. With Smith gone, tensions quickly grew between the colonists and the Powhatans. Sometime around 1612, the new leader of Jamestown, Samuel Argall, tricked Pocahontas into boarding a ship and took her to Jamestown as a **hostage**, or a person who is held prisoner. While in Jamestown, Pocahontas learned British customs, became a Christian, and was given the name Rebecca.

A new life

In 1613, Pocahontas married a tobacco farmer named John Rolfe. Their marriage encouraged peace and friendship between the Powhatans and the colonists for a short while. In 1616, Pocahontas sailed to England with her husband, her baby son Thomas, and several Powhatan men and women. Their arrival in England created a stir. People were curious to see and hear about the Native "princess." She was presented to King James and his court and had her portrait painted. While in England, Pocahontas became gravely ill. She died in 1617.

The European settlers in Jamestown thought Pocahontas was a princess because her father was a powerful chief.

While in England, Pocahontas dressed and behaved like an English gentlewoman.

Sacagawea: guide and interpreter

The goals of the Lewis and Clark expedition were to map rivers, find a waterway linking the Atlantic and Pacific Oceans, and open up the West to American trade.

Sacagawea (Sacajawea) is famous for helping the American explorers Meriwether Lewis and William Clark cross the Rocky Mountains and reach the Pacific Ocean. The Lewis and Clark expedition, known as the Corps of Discovery, was the first group of American explorers to travel west of the Mississippi River. The explorers journeyed thousands of miles and made maps of the land and rivers they saw. Without the help of Sacagawea, it is unlikely that they would have been able to complete their trip safely to the Pacific and back.

Helping the explorers

Sacagawea was born around 1788 in present-day Idaho. She was a Shoshone who was taken from her nation around the age of twelve by the Hidatsas, a warring nation. Her new home was along the upper Missouri River in present-day North Dakota. There, Sacagawea met and married a French Canadian fur trapper named Toussaint Charbonneau. In 1804, Lewis and Clark hired the couple to be their interpreters. Sacagawea spoke Shoshone, Charbonneau spoke French, and both spoke Hidatsa. Lewis and Clark knew that when they reached the Rocky Mountains, they would need to trade with the Shoshones for horses in order to continue their journey. They realized that Sacagawea would be able to help them make the trade. Sacagawea did, in fact, secure horses from the Shoshones, an act that helped ensure the expedition's success. Sacagawea also contributed in other unexpected ways.

*Sacagawea often carried her baby son, Jean Baptiste, in a **cradleboard** on her back. Clark nicknamed the baby "Pomp."*

Leading the way

When the expedition reached Shoshone territory, Sacagawea proved to be a very helpful guide. She remembered trails that she had followed as a child and pointed them out to the explorers. Clark called Sacagawea his "pilot."

Peaceful travels

As the explorers traveled west, they met people from several nations who had never seen Europeans before. Without the presence of Sacagawea and her baby, the Native peoples might have mistaken the expedition for a war party and attacked the group. Since women and children never traveled with war parties, the nations knew that the group was peaceful. Sacagawea also kept the men from starving because she was familiar with local plants. When food was scarce, she found wild foods such as roots and berries.

In her honor

The explorers were so impressed with Sacagawea that they named a river after her. Today, there are several rivers and lakes named after Sacagawea, and there are more than 23 statues in her honor—more than there are of any other woman in the United States. In 2000, the United States government issued a coin honoring her. The coin shows a likeness of Sacagawea carrying her son on her back.

Taking a stand

When European settlers began arriving in the early 1600s, each Native nation had its own distinct homeland. Many Native peoples did not believe that land could be owned as private property. European settlers did not share the same beliefs, however, and they soon began claiming land and forcing Native people off their traditional territories. Tensions between settlers and Native nations lasted for hundreds of years, as settlers slowly moved west across North America. Many Native leaders became famous for their attempts to protect their traditional territories from settlers. Some leaders united their people and battled for their land. Others tried to save their land by negotiating **treaties**, or agreements. The following ten pages highlight some of these famous leaders.

Pontiac's Rebellion

Pontiac, a leader of the Ottawa nation, is famous for uniting several nations in an attempt to stop the British from taking over Native territories. In the mid 1700s, British settlers began moving into the Great Lakes region. Pontiac was angered that the newcomers did not respect his people or their land. He called for the nations in the area to meet at a council, at which he urged them to protect their land and traditional ways of life. He believed that, together, the nations could defeat the British.

He made a plan to launch surprise attacks against British forts around the Great Lakes. During the spring and summer of 1763, warriors from the Ottawa, Ojibwa, Potawatomi, Delaware, Seneca, Miami, Shawnee, and Huron nations defeated eight British forts. Pontiac's Rebellion was the largest victory a group of Native nations had ever won against the British.

*Pontiac was a famous speaker and **strategist**, or planner. He convinced several nations to set aside their differences and work together.*

Ally to the British

Joseph Brant (Thayendanegea) was a famous Mohawk chief, negotiator, and war leader who fought in the American Revolution during the 1770s and early 1780s. The British government promised Brant that it would return Native territories taken by British settlers in present-day New York if Native warriors helped the British soldiers win the Revolution. Brant believed that uniting with the British was the only way to save his people's lands. In 1776, he used his position as a war chief to convince members of the Haudenosaunee Confederacy, including the Mohawks, Onondagas, Cayugas, and Senecas, to fight alongside the British. Although the British eventually lost the war, Brant is known for leading several successful battles.

Unlike many chiefs, Brant learned to speak and write English and studied European history and literature.

Osceola

Osceola was a famous warrior of the Seminole nation in present-day Florida. In 1835, the U.S. government offered a treaty to the Seminoles. The treaty forced them to move from their territories in Florida to **reservations** in Oklahoma. According to Seminole oral tradition, when the United States government presented the treaty, Osceola slashed it with his knife. He was jailed for the action but managed to escape. For the next two years, he led **ambushes**, or surprise attacks, against settlers and government representatives. In 1837, an army officer named General Thomas Jesup called a **truce**, or a temporary stop to the fighting, and lured Osceola to a peace talk. There was no peace talk, however. Osceola was put in prison, where he died a few months later.

News of Osceola's death in 1838 was reported on the front pages of newspapers around the world.

Tecumseh and The Prophet

Tecumseh urged Native nations to work as a group in order to defend their land and ways of life.

The Prophet attracted followers with his spiritual ideas, which encouraged a return to traditional ways.

Two Shawnee brothers, Tecumseh and The Prophet (Tenskwatawa), are famous for uniting Native nations in present-day Ohio. They attempted to stop the invasion of American settlers, goods, and values. By the late 1700s, American settlers were moving into the traditional territories of many nations, including those of the Shawnee, Miami, and Ottawa. In 1795, several nations signed the Treaty of Fort Greenville, which turned over some of their lands to the U.S. government. As settlers moved into the region, they traded alcohol, guns, clothing, and other goods with the Native peoples. American trappers hunted so many animals that it became difficult for Native hunters to find enough animals to support their families. The traditional ways of Native people were in danger of disappearing.

Prophetstown

Tecumseh and The Prophet attracted many followers by encouraging Native people to practice traditional customs. They urged them to avoid contact with settlers, to stop drinking alcohol, to hunt with bows and arrows instead of guns, and to give up their use of American clothing and tools. The brothers also wanted the nations to work together to protect the interests of all Native peoples, not just those of one or two nations. In about 1805, Tecumseh and The Prophet set up a settlement in western Indiana, where their followers could gather. The village became known as Prophetstown. Thousands of Native peoples, including members of the Shawnee, Huron, Ottawa, Kickapoo, Delaware, and Ojibwa nations, lived in Prophetstown.

The settlers grow uneasy

The Native people living in Prophetstown were not hostile toward the settlers in the area, but many American settlers were still concerned about Prophetstown's rapid growth. They feared the power of Tecumseh and his followers. In 1811, the governor of Indiana Territory, William Henry Harrison, led 1,000 soldiers into Prophetstown to drive out the Native people. Harrison's soldiers defeated the Native warriors and then burned Prophetstown to the ground, forcing the people who lived there to scatter to the woods. After Prophetstown was destroyed, its former residents no longer had a place to practice their traditional ways of life.

The Battle of the Little Bighorn

Sitting Bull (Tatanka Iyotanka) and Crazy Horse (Tashunca-uitco) are two Lakota leaders who are famous for trying to protect their nation's territories. They led a famous battle against the U.S. Army—the Battle of the Little Bighorn—to defend their traditional lands.

Broken promises

Sitting Bull was not just a warrior. Within his group, the Hunkpapa Lakota, he was a respected medicine man and spiritual leader. He was also one of the leaders who negotiated the Fort Laramie Treaty with the U.S. government in 1868. The treaty made the Black Hills, which were sacred to the Lakota, off-limits to settlers, miners, and other Americans. In 1874, however, General George Custer led a large group of people into the hills and found gold. **Prospectors**, or people looking for gold, rushed into the Black Hills. The government tried to buy the territory, but the Lakotas refused to sell. The government then broke the Fort Laramie Treaty and warned that any Lakotas who did not move to reservations by 1876 would have to fight the army. The Lakotas stayed to defend their land.

Visions of victory

In March 1876, the U.S. Army moved into Lakota territory. Native groups in the area were angry and realized that they would have to fight together to protect their land. People of the Cheyenne, Arapaho, and Lakota nations gathered to perform a Sun Dance ceremony and prepare for battle. After leading the Sun Dance, Sitting Bull had a vision of soldiers falling headfirst into a valley. People thought the vision was a sign that they would defeat the army.

A short triumph

On June 25, 1876, Custer led troops into the valley of the Little Bighorn River to attack Native groups who were camping there, including those led by Sitting Bull and Crazy Horse. Custer and his soldiers believed that they would easily defeat the Native leaders and their warriors, but the Native groups won the battle. Although they were victorious, Sitting Bull, Crazy Horse, and their followers were chased by the army, until they surrendered in 1877.

Sitting Bull's surrender
In 1877, Sitting Bull led about 200 of his followers to Canada to avoid the U.S. Army. They spent four years there, but it became difficult to find enough buffalo to hunt. In 1881, Sitting Bull and his followers returned to the United States to surrender.

© CRAZY HORSE MEM. FND.

The Crazy Horse Memorial in the Black Hills is a huge sculpture based on detailed descriptions from people who knew what Crazy Horse looked like. The sculpture is a work-in-progress.

Crazy Horse
Even before the Battle of the Little Bighorn, Crazy Horse was known among his people as a brave leader and warrior. He was always committed to protecting the Lakota land and way of life. After the U.S. Army made him surrender in 1877, he refused to sign a treaty. Although he was forced onto a reservation, he never accepted the rules and refused to seek permission to come and go.

Louis Riel

Louis Riel, a renowned **Métis** political leader, is often regarded as the **founder**, or "father," of the province of Manitoba. He is famous for trying to prevent the Canadian government from taking over Métis lands during the mid to late 1800s. He is also known for protecting the rights and culture of the Métis.

Guilty of treason

In 1875, Riel was **banished** from Canada, or forced to leave the country, for executing a Canadian prisoner named Thomas Scott. In 1884, however, a group of Métis from Saskatchewan asked Riel to return to Canada and help them negotiate with the government. Riel agreed, on the condition that they would avoid violence. Fighting broke out at Duck Lake in present-day Saskatchewan just one year later, however, creating hostility between the Métis and the Canadians. After a four-day battle at Batoche, Riel was arrested, tried, and found guilty of **treason**, or betraying his country. He was hanged in 1885, in Regina, Saskatchewan.

Red River

Even as a young man, Riel was committed to fighting for Métis rights and lands. For many years, the Métis hunted and farmed in the Red River region of present-day Winnipeg, Manitoba. When the region was sold to the Canadian government in 1869, the Métis realized that they would soon be pushed off their land. They knew that they needed to make decisions for themselves to protect their rights and way of life. Louis Riel was a well-known and determined Métis leader, so the people turned to him for help.

Riel's provisional government

Riel established a **provisional**, or temporary, Métis government, which created a List of Rights for the people. The list included the rights to stay on their land, to practice their religion freely, and to be involved in any decisions relating to Red River. Members of Riel's government negotiated with the Canadian government until it agreed to most of the Métis List of Rights. In 1870, Manitoba joined the Canadian confederation and became a province.

Chief Joseph

Chief Joseph (Hin-mah-too-yah-lat-kekt) is famous for leading one of the most amazing **retreats** in American history. His people, the Nez Perce, eluded U.S. soldiers over a distance of 1,700 miles (2735 km).

Standing firm

Chief Joseph became leader of the Nez Perce after his father, Joseph the Elder, died in 1871. In 1877, the U.S. Army ordered the Nez Perce to move from their vast reservation in present-day Oregon and Idaho to a smaller area of land in western Idaho. The new reservation was only one-tenth the size of the original. Although Joseph did not want to move, he realized that his people could not defeat the army. The Nez Perce agreed to leave, and Joseph began preparing to lead them to the new reservation.

Leading the retreat

Before the group left, however, twenty warriors attacked nearby settlers out of anger. The attack quickly sent 2,000 soldiers after Joseph's group. Joseph knew his people were outnumbered, so he avoided the soldiers. He led nearly 700 people across Idaho and Montana to try to reach Canada, where the army could not follow. After three months, Joseph's group was close to Canada, but they faced starvation and harsh weather. Joseph had to surrender to ensure the safety of his people.

The U.S. government promised that if Chief Joseph surrendered, he could return to his homeland. Joseph rode to surrender on October 5, 1877, but the government did not keep its promise. He and his people were sent to reservations in Kansas and Oklahoma.

Cochise and Geronimo

Cochise and Geronimo (Goyathlay) are two of the best-known Apache leaders in history. In the mid to late 1800s, they fought to keep living in their Apache homelands in the Southwest as more and more American settlers arrived.

Wrongly accused

At first, Cochise and the Chiricahua Apaches lived peacefully with the Americans who settled in Apache territory. Cochise even allowed a stagecoach company to build a station in Apache Pass. The peaceful relations did not last long, however. In 1861, a U.S. Army lieutenant named George N. Bascom wrongly accused Cochise of stealing cattle and kidnapping a settler's son. Cochise and a few of his men visited Bascom to convince him of Cochise's innocence.

Bascom immediately tried to arrest Cochise and his men. Cochise escaped and took several settlers hostage in order to trade for the release of his warriors. Bascom and Cochise both killed their prisoners, however, sparking a series of wars between the U.S. Army and the Apache warriors. The series of wars, sometimes known as the Apache wars, lasted more than 25 years.

The Apaches unite

Cochise's followers were joined by the Membreno Apaches and the White Mountain Apaches. Together, the groups tried to drive Americans out of Apache lands. Before his death in 1874, Cochise and his warriors raided several American settlements and stopped settlers from using the Apache Pass, making it difficult for the newcomers to take over Apache territory.

Geronimo takes the lead

After Cochise's death, Geronimo led the Apaches in defending their lands. He fought settlers, who were taking over Apache territories, and the U.S. Army, which was ordering the Apaches to move from their homelands onto reservations. In 1875, after years of fighting, the U.S. government forced more than 4,000 Apaches, including Geronimo, to move to the San Carlos Reservation in present-day eastern Arizona.

Escape to the mountains

In 1876, Geronimo and about 50 of his followers left San Carlos and escaped to the mountains of Mexico. A U.S. general, George Crook, traveled to Mexico to pursue them. He used Apache **scouts**, or guides, to help him track Geronimo throughout the harsh territory. During the final months of the chase, there were more than 5,000 American soldiers trailing Geronimo and his followers. In 1882, the scouts located Geronimo, and he agreed to return to the reservation along with his people. After three years, he became restless and escaped once again with more than 100 followers. They were pursued by the army for four years. In 1886, Geronimo finally surrendered to General Nelson Miles. The Apaches were split up and sent to reservations in present-day Florida, Alabama, and Oklahoma, where they were forced to give up their traditional way of life.

Although Geronimo was not a chief, many Apache chiefs respected him because he was a bold and determined leader. He was one of the last Native leaders to surrender to the United States government.

Geronimo and his people knew the mountains well and were able to hide from the U.S. Army for almost ten years.

Striving for peace

Rather than fighting, some Native leaders worked to secure peace between their people and the settlers in the late 1700s and the mid 1800s. These leaders believed that their nations could not stop the wave of settlers and that fighting would only lead to death and sorrow. These Native people are famous for trying to negotiate and solve problems peacefully, even though the governments often broke their agreements.

A brave woman

Nancy (Nan'yehi) Ward, a Cherokee woman who lived in present-day Tennessee, is famous for trying to maintain peaceful relations between her people and the U.S. government. As a young woman, Nancy showed great courage in a battle with the neighboring Creeks. To reward her bravery, the Cherokees selected her as *Ghighau*, or Beloved Woman. This powerful and highly respected position made Ward the head of the Women's Council and allowed her to vote on the Council of Chiefs.

A plea for peace

Ward used her position to promote peace between the Cherokees and the settlers. She believed that there could be friendship between Native and American women. She spoke with representatives of the U.S. government on behalf of her people and participated in several treaty negotiations. In later years, after the government broke its treaties with the Cherokee, Ward cautioned her people about selling more land to the settlers.

Nancy Ward was well known and respected by settlers moving into Cherokee territory. She often warned American settlers of attacks planned by Cherokee warriors.

Chief Crowfoot

Crowfoot (Isapo-muxika), who became a chief of the Blackfoot nation in about 1869, was a revered leader and negotiator. He is famous for trying to protect his people's rights and for ensuring the safety of the Blackfoot in present-day Calgary, Alberta. Crowfoot was born around 1830 into the Blood nation of the Blackfoot Confederacy, which also included the Peigan, Northern Blackfoot, Sarcee, and Gros Ventres nations. Although he was a skilled warrior and fought bravely in several battles with other nations, Crowfoot was well known for protecting his people and trying to avoid violence whenever possible. During the 1870s, thousands of settlers arrived in Alberta, taking over Native territories and hunting herds of buffalo.

The Canadian government soon wanted to build a large railroad on Blackfoot land. Chief Crowfoot wanted to protect his land, but he was also determined to live peacefully with the settlers. He tried to establish friendly relations with fur traders and **missionaries** who were settling in Blackfoot territories, but he also advised his people against drinking the alcohol offered by the settlers and traders. Chief Crowfoot signed a treaty in 1877 that gave up a vast amount of Blackfoot territory in order to maintain peace. Not long after he signed the treaty, however, the Blackfoot nation faced starvation because very few buffalo lived on the territory allotted to them in the treaty. To ensure his people's survival, Chief Crowfoot took them to a **reserve**.

*Chief Crowfoot was a great **orator**, or speaker. This painting shows him speaking to Governor General the Marquis of Lorne at a meeting at Blackfoot Crossing, Alberta, in the early 1880s.*

Hope in hard times

Life was very hard for the people of many nations in the late 1700s and throughout the 1800s. As settlers moved west, they introduced alcohol, guns, and new diseases to the Native nations. Thousands of Native people died as a result. The survivors lost their land to the settlers and were forced to live on reservations. Sickness, sadness, and hopelessness spread throughout many nations. During these hard times, spiritual leaders emerged who inspired their people to have hope and to take pride in their traditional ways and cultures. These leaders are famous for guiding and advising their people. They are known as **prophets**. They include The Prophet (see pages 14-15), Handsome Lake, and Wovoka (the Ghost Dance Prophet).

The Code of Handsome Lake

By the late 1700s, the once-strong Haudenosaunee nations were weakened by diseases, alcohol, and loss of lands. In 1799, a Seneca man named Handsome Lake had a series of visions that warned Native people to return to their traditional values, or they would suffer even more. Based on his visions, he created the Code of Handsome Lake, which described the rules by which people should live. He believed that people should avoid alcohol, live peacefully, take up farming, and refuse to give up any more land to the settlers. Handsome Lake traveled to reservations to teach Native people about the new religion, known as the Longhouse Religion. His code reminded them of the value of land, family, and community.

Wovoka's vision

By the late 1800s, most western nations were forced onto reservations, where there was little food. Many people became sick, including a Paiute man named Wovoka. When he recovered from his illness, Wovoka stated that he had been taken to the spirit world and given an important message for his people. The message stated that the earth would soon die and be reborn as it was before the settlers arrived. Wovoka encouraged people to live peacefully with one another. He also advised them to prepare for the new world by performing the Ghost Dance. He and his followers meditated, prayed, chanted, and danced to bring back their old way of life and their relatives who had died.

The Ghost Dance

Like Handsome Lake, Wovoka stressed the importance of practicing Native traditions and advised his followers against drinking alcohol. American settlers feared that the Ghost Dance religion might lead to violence against them. The government tried to ban the Ghost Dance in 1890. When followers of the religion ignored the ban and gathered near Wounded Knee to perform the Ghost Dance, American soldiers killed more than 300 of them. Despite this massacre at Wounded Knee, Wovoka's religion helped renew pride and hope for Native people and many continued to practice the religion. A form of the Ghost Dance is still performed by some Lakota today.

Wovoka's new religion and its dance soon spread across the West. People from many nations, including the Cheyenne, the Arapaho, and the Lakota, practiced the Ghost Dance religion.

Preserving cultures

Unlike Europeans, most Native nations did not record their histories using written words. Instead, they used **pictographs** and oral traditions of stories and songs to pass their history and spiritual beliefs from one **generation** to the next. In the 1800s, however, the governments of Canada and the United States made it illegal for people on reservations to speak Native languages, to practice traditional ways, and to teach children the histories of their nations. Some people became famous for striving to preserve Native cultures and traditions.

Sequoyah's gift

Most Native languages did not have a written alphabet because people had never needed one. A Cherokee man named Sequoyah became interested in the letters and books he saw settlers reading. He soon realized that the pages contained words. Sequoyah believed that if his people could write down their laws and history, they could convince the U.S. government that they were an independent nation with a right to keep their land. Sequoyah set to work creating a method of writing down the Cherokee language. It took twelve years, but in 1821 he completed the Cherokee **syllabary**. A syllabary is a list of written symbols. Each symbol represents a **syllable**, or a group of letters that forms part of a word's sound.

Powerful words
Sequoyah was the first person in history to create an entire syllabary by himself. Sequoyah's syllabary was so easy to learn that thousands of Cherokees could read and write in their language within months of its invention. They soon created newspapers, books, and a constitution in Cherokee. Sequoyah's syllabary allowed his people to record and save their history, culture, and spiritual beliefs.

Poet and performer

Emily Pauline Johnson, a talented Mohawk woman, was a famous poet and performer during the late 1800s. She was born in 1861 and grew up near Brantford, Ontario. By the 1890s, she was reciting poems about her Native heritage to audiences in Ontario. Johnson became very popular and began performing to large audiences in eastern Canada, the United States, and England. Johnson's costumes and the manner in which she performed her poems fascinated her audiences. During her years as a performer, she also published several books, including a book of Native stories told to her by a Squamish chief.

Hopi pottery

In the late 1800s, a Hopi woman named Nampeyo became famous for **reviving**, or bringing back, a style of Hopi pottery that was once made in a large, ancient Hopi village called Sityatki. Nampeyo mimicked designs she saw on the old jars and bowls but used different types of clay when shaping her own pottery. Nampeyo instructed her three daughters, two granddaughters, and niece on how to make the pottery. She would often shape a pot and give it to the young girls, who then painted on the designs.

Johnson was known for wearing two different costumes while performing. During the first half of a performance, she wore an evening gown. For the second part, however, she wore Native clothing, including a buckskin dress and a necklace made of bear claws.

Today's famous people

Today, many Native North Americans are famous for trying to make a difference in the lives of all Native people. Some are known for their talents and achievements. Others are well-known spokespeople for their nations.

Russell Means

Russell Means is a famous Oglala Lakota activist, author, and actor. He was born at the Pine Ridge Indian Reservation in South Dakota. In the 1970s, he became the first national director of an important organization called the American Indian Movement (AIM), which works to protect the rights of Native peoples. He has led thousands of protesters and has helped bring attention to the many problems faced by Native peoples, both in the past and in the present. He continues to fight for freedom and the preservation of Native American cultures and traditions.

Acclaimed Navajo artist
R.C. Gorman is one of today's best-known Navajo artists. He was born in Arizona on the Navajo Reservation in 1931. He has won numerous awards, and his work is collected by museums all over the world, including the National Museum of the American Indian and the Metropolitan Museum of Art. Today, he owns the Navajo Gallery in Taos, New Mexico. One of his paintings, entitled *Night Stories*, is shown above.

Buffy Sainte-Marie

Besides being a successful singer, songwriter, and artist, Buffy Sainte-Marie is also a well-known spokeswoman for Native rights and education. In 1969, she founded the Nihewan Foundation for Native American Education. The foundation helps improve education for Native people and teaches non-Native people about Native cultures. Sainte-Marie has also recorded more than seventeen albums and has performed her music in places all over the world, including Europe and Asia.

Buffy Sainte-Marie was born on a Cree reserve in Qu'Appelle Valley, Saskatchewan. She was adopted and raised in Maine and Massachusetts.

Robbie Robertson

Robbie Robertson is a Mohawk singer and songwriter who was born in Toronto, Ontario. He was a member of the rock group, The Band, for over ten years. In 1994, The Band was inducted into the Rock and Roll Hall of Fame in Cleveland, Ohio for its achievements. In the same year, Robertson began playing with the Native American group, The Red Road Ensemble. Together, the group's members created a collection of songs for a television series that told the history of Native Americans.

Wilma Mankiller

Wilma Mankiller became the first woman to act as chief of a large nation—the Cherokee nation—when she was elected in 1985. She was the nation's principal chief until 1995. During that time, she helped make many positive changes in her community, such as creating jobs and improving health care. Her leadership has had a positive effect on many members of the Cherokee nation. For her accomplishments, she was inducted into the Women's Hall of Fame in New York City in 1994.

After being elected chief, Wilma Mankiller created the Institute for Cherokee Literacy, which helps her people preserve their language and traditions.

Native North American firsts

Jim Thorpe was the first president of the American Professional Football Association. Today, the association is known as the National Football League (NFL).

Many Native people have become famous for being the first to make great accomplishments in sports, performing arts, politics, or art. These pages highlight just a few of these impressive people.

Jim Thorpe

Some sports historians believe that Jim Thorpe, a member of the Sauk and Fox nations, was one of the most talented athletes in history. He represented the United States at the 1912 Olympics, where he won gold medals in the decathlon and pentathlon. His victories marked the first time that one person had ever won both events at the Olympic Games. Thorpe also excelled at several other sports, including football and baseball.

Sarah Winnemucca

In 1883, a Paiute woman named Sarah Winnemucca published a book about her life called *Life Among the Paiutes: Their Wrongs and Claims*. The book was the first ever to be written and published by a Native woman. Winnemucca also founded the first school for Native American children in 1884.

The Cherokee Phoenix
After Sequoyah invented the Cherokee syllabary, the Cherokee nation was able to start printing a newspaper called the *Cherokee Phoenix*, which was the first Native newspaper in North America. It was also the first newspaper to be published in a Native language. The first issue was printed on February 28, 1828.

Annie Dodge Wauneka

A Navajo woman named Annie Dodge Wauneka worked for many years to educate her people about preventing and treating American and European diseases, especially tuberculosis. In 1963, she became the first Native person to be presented with the Presidential Medal of Freedom.

Maria and Marjorie Tallchief

As young girls, Maria and Marjorie Tallchief dreamed of becoming ballerinas. When George Balanchine formed the New York City Ballet in 1948, Maria became the company's **prima balerina**, or leading female dancer. She was the first American to receive the title of prima ballerina. Marjorie danced with the Paris Opéra Ballet for five years. She performed for presidents, kings, and queens. In 1980, Maria and Marjorie Tallchief founded the Chicago City Ballet.

Maria Tallchief received many awards and honors during her career, including the Indian Achievement Award and an honorary lifetime membership in the Indian Council Fire.

Susan LaFlesche

Susan LaFlesche was born on the Omaha Reservation in Nebraska on June 17, 1865. She was the first Native woman to earn a medical degree and work as a doctor. After graduating from medical school in 1889, she returned to Nebraska and traveled to many reservations, where she treated people who were sick. She worked hard to improve the Omaha nation's health care. LaFlesche also organized a campaign to build the Thurston County Medical Association, a hospital for people in the town of Walthill, Nebraska. The hospital opened in 1913.

Glossary

Note: Boldfaced words that are defined in the book may not appear in the glossary

Algonkian A group of related Native languages spoken by the majority of Native nations along the East coast

alliance An association of two or more groups that is formed to achieve a common purpose or goal

constitution A written document that contains the laws and plans of a particular government

council A group of representatives called together to give advice, discuss problems, or make decisions for their people

cradleboard A board or frame on which a baby is bundled

generation A step or level in a family, such as the children, the parents, or the grandparents

Iroquoian A group of related Native languages spoken by the majority of Native nations in the Great Lakes region of Canada and the United States

Métis The group of people with Native ancestors and French-Canadian or other non-Native ancestors

missionary A religious person who travels from place to place to convert people to a different faith

negotiator A person who works with others in order to reach decisions or resolve differences

oral tradition The stories that are passed down verbally from one generation to the next about a group of people and its history

pictograph A picture or drawing that represents a word or an idea

prophet A person who gives others an important message or tells what will happen in the future

reservation (reserve) A specific area of land set aside for Native people by a government

retreat The act of moving away from a dangerous place or situation

territory An area of land on which a group of people traditionally lived

Index

32

1 2 3 4 5 6 7 8 9 0 Printed in the U.S.A. 3 2 1 0 9 8 7 6 5 4